PUFFALUMPS™

BEDTIME STORYBOOK

Hippo Books
Scholastic Publications Limited
London

PUFFALUMPS BEDTIME STORYBOOK: 1

Scholastic Publications Ltd.,
10 Earlham Street, London WC2H 9RX, UK.

Scholastic Inc.,
730 Broadway, New York, NY 10003, USA.

Scholastic Tab Publications Ltd.,
123 Newkirk Road, Richmond Hill,
Ontario L4C 3G5, Canada.

Ashton Scholastic Pty. Ltd.,
PO Box 579, Gosford, New South Wales,
Australia.

Ashton Scholastic Ltd.,
165 Marua Road, Panmure, Auckland 6,
New Zealand.

First published by Scholastic Publications Ltd., 1988.

Design and illustration by Brown, Wells and Jacobs Ltd., London.

ISBN 0 590 70829 5

Made and printed by Printer Industria Gráfica S.A., Barcelona
Typeset in Surrey by Words & Pictures Limited

PUFFALUMPS™

PAINT THEIR HOME

All the Puffalumps live together in Puffalump House. They each have their own bedroom, and there is a big sitting-room with soft comfy chairs, and a big kitchen with a table in the middle.

The Puffalumps are very proud of their home and they try to keep it looking clean and tidy, even though sometimes things do not get put away!

One Spring day Bunny and Puppy were in the sitting-room cleaning and polishing. Bunny was dusting the shelves and window ledges, and Puppy was spraying them with polish so that everything gleamed in the sunshine.

"Not much more to do now," said Bunny as she carefully dusted the mantlepiece above the fireplace.

"That's good — all this housework is harder than it looks!" replied Puppy.

"I'll just give this picture frame a good dusting, and then we'll have finished," said Bunny.

She reached up and lifted the picture off the hook over the fireplace. It was one of the Puffalumps' favourites and showed a field full of bright red poppies.

As Bunny began to dust the wooden frame around the picture she noticed something funny had happened to the wall!

"Come and look at the wall," said Bunny.

The two Puffalumps stood in front of the fireplace and looked at the place where the picture had been. The wallpaper was just the same — but much, much brighter!

"How strange," said Puppy, "the paper behind the picture has got brighter!"

Bunny looked at the square patch where the picture had been, and then at the wallpaper in the rest of the sitting-room.

"No, Puppy — the wallpaper behind the picture hasn't got brighter. All the other wallpaper has faded!" said Bunny sadly.

"Oh dear," sighed Puppy. "Well I suppose it has been on the wall for a long time."

"I know. I've had an idea. We'll redecorate the sitting-room and put new wallpaper up!" said Bunny.

"And we can paint the door and window frames as well!" said Puppy.

Bunny and Puppy went off to tell the other Puffalumps about the picture frame and the bright patch on the wall.

"We could have purple wallpaper and yellow paint on the doors and windows!" suggested Kitty.

The other Puffalumps looked horrified at the thought of purple and yellow together.

"I don't think that would look very nice!" said Bear Cub. "We should have black wallpaper and dark brown paint," he added.

"But that would be so dark and gloomy," said Cow, who liked bright colours.

In a moment all the Puffalumps were talking at once, arguing about which colours looked the nicest.

"Quiet!" said Mouse. "I have an idea." All the Puffalumps stopped talking and listened to Mouse.

"Now then," said Mouse, "we all like the colours we already have in the sitting-room, don't we?"

The Puffalumps nodded. The blue flowery wallpaper and white paint had been there a long time, but they did like it!

"Well, why don't we have the same again?" asked Mouse.

The Puffalumps thought about Mouse's idea for a minute. The longer they thought, the more they agreed it was an excellent idea, particularly as they couldn't decide on a new colour.

Cow and Kitty went off to the shops to buy the wallpaper and white paint, and the brushes and wallpaper paste.

The other Puffalumps went into the sitting-room and began to move the furniture away from the wall so they could get to work on the papering and the painting. Puppy and Bear Cub found some old sheets in a cupboard upstairs and covered the tables and chairs to stop them getting covered in paint.

In no time at all Cow and Kitty were back from the shops with rolls of wallpaper, pots of paint and a bag of brushes.

"Right! Let us get started," said Puppy.

"What do we do first?" asked Bear Cub.

"Well what did we do first last time?" asked Mouse.

"I didn't — I mean I have never done this before!" said Bear Cub. "Have you?"

Mouse shook her head and the Puffalumps realized that none of them had ever painted anything, or put up wallpaper, before!

"I don't think it can be that difficult!" said Kitty. "It's easy to paint the doors and window frames, and there are instructions in the bag for putting up wallpaper!"

Not all the Puffalumps thought it was going to be as easy as Kitty seemed to think, but they set to work anyway.

Bunny and Cow began pulling the old wallpaper off the walls, while Bear Cub and Mouse mixed the wallpaper paste with water and laid out the new wallpaper on a table.

Kitty and Puppy sandpapered all the old paint off the sitting-room door and the big window frame and then carefully began to paint.

"This paint is very runny!" said Puppy, trying to stop drops dripping off his brush.

"Try not to put so much paint on the brush," said Kitty, bossily.

But just as she reached up to paint the top of the door a big blob of paint dripped off her brush and landed right on the end of her nose!

"You do look funny, Kitty!" laughed Puppy. Kitty crossed her eyes to try and see the blob of white paint on the end of her nose which made her look even funnier. The Puffalumps laughed as Puppy wiped the blob of paint away with an old rag.

By now Bunny and Cow had taken the old wallpaper off one wall and Bear Cub and Mouse had spread the sticky paste on the back of the new wallpaper.

"Here we go!" said Bear Cub, carefully lifting a long strip of wallpaper off the table.

"Oh, do be careful, Bear Cub, it's very sticky," said Mouse. And just as Mouse said that, Bear Cub slipped and fell, wrapping himself in the sticky wallpaper.

"I think you should hold the paper the other way round the next time," said Mouse, "then you can stick it straight onto the wall, and not on yourself!"

And Mouse was right. The next time Bear Cub picked up a strip of wallpaper, the sticky side was facing the wall and not him! And this time it stuck to the wall!

They worked very hard all day, and by evening the new wallpaper was up on the walls, and the door and window frames were brightly painted.

The Puffalumps were very tired, but after supper, as they sat quietly in their sitting-room, they felt very pleased.

"It was a bit more difficult than I thought," said Kitty.

"But it was worth it," said Bear Cub, and all the Puffalumps agreed.

PUFFALUMPS™

AND THE DOLPHIN

On hot, summer days the Puffalumps love to go to the beach. They pack their towels, buckets and spades into their bright red car and drive to the seaside.

One very hot and sunny day all the Puffalumps were on the beach. Bear Cub and Cow were lying on towels counting seagulls. Kitty, Bunny and Puppy were playing in the sea, running in and out of the shallow water kicking it up into the air and laughing.

"This water's so warm it's like a bath!" shouted Bunny as a wave splashed over his legs.

"Yes, but it is cooler than just lying on the beach," said Kitty, who thought it was a very hot day indeed.

"Come on in, Mouse, it's great fun," shouted Puppy, waving at Mouse who was sitting nearby.

"No thanks, Puppy. I am having a lovely time just sitting here watching the sea," replied Mouse.

“But it’s lovely — come and play with us,” Kitty and Bunny called together.

Mouse just shook her head and kept on watching the waves. The other Puffalumps thought this very strange. Mouse usually liked to play games as much as any of them and always joined in!

Mouse kept quiet for a moment and then replied: “Well, you see, I don’t know how to swim, and I am a bit nervous of going in the sea, even with all of you around.”

“You mean you’ve never been taught to swim?” said Kitty, surprised.

“That’s right,” replied Mouse. “I’ve wanted to learn to swim for ages, but there have been so many other things to do instead!”

Kitty went to tell the other Puffalumps that Mouse wanted to learn to swim — and they decided to start to teach her right away.

Kitty brought Mouse a rubber ring which she put round her waist and blew up. “That will keep you afloat Mouse. You won’t have to worry about sinking!” said Kitty.

Mouse walked down the beach as the Puffalumps shouted encouragement to her.

“Don’t worry Mouse, the water is lovely and warm,” said Puppy.

“Yes, and there are hardly any waves today,” added Cow.

Even with the other Puffalumps nearby Mouse was still nervous! But she bravely waded into the sea until it was up to her waist.

“What do I do now?” she asked.

“I’ll show you,” said Bear Cub, who was one of the best swimmers.

“Now then Mouse, just lie down in the water — the rubber ring will hold you up, and so will I!” said Bear Cub.

Very carefully Mouse lay down in the water, and Bear Cub told her to start moving her arms and legs.

"Kick your legs, Mouse and use your arms as well — pretend you are trying to grab hold of the sea and pull it towards you!" said Bear Cub.

Mouse kicked and kicked, and moved her arms through the water. As she did so she felt herself begin to move.

"Whoo! I think I am swimming, Bear Cub!" shouted Mouse in excitement.

"You see what fun it is!" said Bear Cub.

But as Bear Cub walked slowly forward holding onto Mouse he put his foot on a slippery rock and fell over!

"Blup!" said Bear Cub as his head went underwater.

"Uggh!" said Mouse as she swallowed a mouthful of salty water.

In a moment Bear Cub found his feet and stood up.

"Urghh . . . that sea water is a bit salty," said Bear Cub shaking his wet head, "but don't worry Mouse, it doesn't do you any harm!"

"Perhaps not, but I think I've had enough swimming practice for one day," said Mouse, wading towards the beach.

But just then all the Puffalumps on the shore started shouting — "Mouse, Bear Cub! Look behind you. There is a big fish in the sea."

Both the Puffalumps looked round and saw a big blue fish. Every now and then it leapt right out of the water before diving deep.

"Oohh, is it a sh . . . sh . . . shark?" asked Mouse nervously.

Bear Cub laughed. "No, Mouse, it is a dolphin. They are very friendly and very clever!"

In a moment the dolphin swam up beside Mouse and Bear Cub. It had a big round nose, a fin on its back which stuck up out of the water, and two friendly eyes.

“Hello Puffalumps!” said the dolphin in a high, squeaky voice. “I heard you splashing about and thought I would come and see what you were doing!”

“Mouse is learning to swim,” explained Bear Cub.

“Learning to swim?” said the dolphin. “I thought everyone knew how to swim. It’s strange that Mouse can’t!”

“Well, we don’t live in the water like you,” said Mouse. “And anyway, it is very wet and very salty!”

“I know, I know. It’s lovely and salty!” said the dolphin.

"I don't think I'll ever learn to swim properly!" said Mouse sadly.

Bear Cub put his arm around Mouse. "Never mind. I am sorry I dropped you, but you can try again soon."

The dolphin, who had been listening very closely, suddenly squeaked loudly and thumped his tail on the sea, splashing Mouse and Bear Cub again!

"I know, I know. I will give Mouse a ride on my back. It is very safe and great fun," said the dolphin.

“That’s very kind of you, dolphin, but I’m not sure,” said Mouse nervously.

“You must have a ride, Mouse,” said Bear Cub excitedly, “it will make you want to learn to swim even more.”

Mouse reluctantly climbed onto the dolphin’s back.

“O.K. dolphin, I am on and holding on,” said Mouse.

“Here we go then!” said the dolphin. He waggled his tail very quickly in the water, and with Mouse holding on tightly he set off.

Soon the dolphin and Mouse were whizzing through the sea.

“Whee!” went Mouse. “This is fun. I never know you could swim so fast, dolphin!”

On the beach, the other Puffalumps watched the dolphin and Mouse until they headed back towards the beach. When the water got very shallow Mouse hopped off.

“That was marvellous, dolphin, thank you ever so much. I’m quite out of breath!” said Mouse.

“That’s all right, that’s all right,” said the dolphin. “I must go now, but I am sure the next time I see you you’ll be swimming by yourself!”

“ ’Bye, ’bye!” shouted the Puffalumps as the dolphin swam quickly away.

"Well. Will you learn how to swim?" asked Kitty.

"Just as soon as I can!" said Mouse as the Puffalumps walked back up the beach.

And next time Mouse met the dolphin she was swimming all by herself!

PUFFALUMPS™

AND THE SNOW

One winter's day the Puffalumps woke up to find that it had snowed heavily in the night. The snow covered everything.

The trees at the bottom of the garden were white and sparkly, and Puffalump Hill looked as if it were wearing a big white sheet.

“What fun we re going to have!” said Bear Cub, with his nose pressed against the frosty window pane.

“Yes, we can take the sledge over to Puffalump Hill!” said Mouse.

The Puffalumps had a lovely hot breakfast of porridge with honey on the top, and then wrapped themselves up warmly in gloves and hats and scarves and boots before going out.

“I’ll go and get the sledge out of the shed,” said Cow, going outside. Kitty went along to help, and the two Puffalumps walked across the snow leaving big footprints behind them.

“Now where is it?” said Cow, peering into the shed. “I think I put it under these old sacks.”

Cow pulled the sacks away and there was the Puffalumps’ wooden sledge — big enough to carry two of the Puffalumps at one time. They pulled the sledge out, and then noticed two strange things leaning against the wall.

“What are those, Cow?” Kitty asked, pointing at the objects.

“They’re skis. Look, I’ll show you,” said Cow, lifting the skis out of the shed.

They were long pieces of wood, smooth and shiny, with some straps in the middle and curved up at the front.

“Your feet go in here,” said Cow, pointing at the straps, “and one ski is buckled onto each foot.”

“I see,” said Kitty. “But why do they curl up at the front?”

“That is so the skis don’t dig into the snow when you are going down hill!” explained Cow.

“Do you think I’d be able to learn to ski?” asked Kitty.

“Of course — if you don’t try to go too fast!” said Cow.

Going back into the shed Cow found two ski sticks as well. She explained to Kitty that you used the sticks to push yourself along, and that the round bits on the bottom of the sticks stopped them sinking too far into the snow.

The two Puffalumps walked back to Puffalump House, Kitty pulling the sledge on a long bit of rope, and Cow carrying the skis and sticks.

Soon they were ready to go off to Puffalump Hill.

"Hold on a moment," said Puppy. "Now we have had our breakfast, I'm going to put the scraps out for the birds."

"That is a good idea, Puppy," said Mouse. "With all the snow around it will be difficult for them to find food."

The Puffalumps took some bread and scattered it on the snow outside their house, and they left a bowl of water as well so the birds would not be thirsty.

The birds came flying down from all the trees around Puffalump House.

"Thank you, Puffalumps," they said. "We didn't think we would get any food today."

The Puffalumps set off happily for Puffalump Hill.

"I know a good slope on Puffalump Hill — it is not too steep, and we'll have a wonderful time with the sledge!" said Puppy.

The Puffalumps waited for Puppy to show them the good slope.

"There it is!" said Puppy pointing at one slope.

"No, wait a minute, it is that one over there," he said, pointing in a different direction.

"Oh dear! I don't know which one it is. With all this snow about everything looks different," said Puppy.

The Puffalumps set off up the slope with Cow pulling the sledge and Kitty carrying the skis.

"Here we are!" said Cow when they reached the top. "Who's coming on the first sledge ride with me?"

All the Puffalumps wanted to go at once, but they decided Kitty should be first because she had helped Cow get the sledge out of the shed.

She stuck the skis she was carrying into the snow, and climbed onto the sledge behind Cow.

"Ready, Kitty?" asked Cow. "Hang on tight."

"I am ready, and I am steady. Let's go!" cried Kitty excitedly.

Both Puffalumps lifted their feet off the ground and the sledge began to move down the slope. Faster and faster it went until Cow could feel the wind whistling past her face!

“Whee . . . this is fun,” shouted Kitty as the sledge whizzed down Puffalump Hill.

When it got to the bottom of the hill the slope was not so steep, and the sledge came to a stop.

“Whew, that was marvellous, wasn’t it Kitty!” said Cow.

“Yes, but now we have to pull the sledge back up the hill so the others can have a go,” said Kitty.

"Never mind," said Cow, "it is not far for so much fun!"

At the top of the slope the other Puffalumps watched Cow and Kitty begin to walk back up.

"I can hardly wait for my turn," said Puppy. "I know. I'll have a go on the skis!"

"Do you know how to use them?" asked Mouse.

"No, but I heard Cow explain where you put your feet. And anyway I don't think it can be that difficult!"

Puppy put the skis on the snow and buckled the straps around his feet.

"Err, Puppy . . ." Mouse said.

"Not now, Mouse!" said Puppy, "I am trying to concentrate on these skis."

"But Puppy . . ." said Mouse again. Puppy was not listening. He finished buckling on the skis and picked up the ski sticks.

"Right, I'm ready — wait a minute, I am going backwards," said a surprised Puppy.

As the other Puffalumps watched, Puppy began to slide down Puffalump Hill — backwards!

"That is what I was trying to tell you, Puppy!" shouted Mouse. "You have put the skis on the wrong way round!"

Puppy looked down at the skis.

"Oh no, what am I going to do now?" said Puppy as he sped backwards down the slope.

Cow and Kitty were trudging back up the slope when Puppy whizzed past them.

"I didn't know that Puppy was a trick skier!" said Kitty.

“I don’t think he is!” said Cow.

Just then Puppy — who couldn’t see where he was going — ran into a snow drift. There was a big puff of snow, and when it settled all the Puffalumps could see were the skis sticking out of the top!

Cow and Kitty ran over. "Are you all right, Puppy?" they asked.

"I think so," said Puppy, as he struggled upright in the snow. "At least the snow is soft!"

The two Puffalumps helped Puppy up.

"I think I should show you how to ski properly," Cow told Puppy, who had to agree!

By the end of the day, all the Puffalumps had had lots of rides on the sledge; and Puppy was skiing down the slope facing the right way!